Madam C.J. Walker

Self-Made Millionaire

Patricia and Fredrick McKissack

Series Consultant: Dr. Russell L. Adams, Chairman,
Afro-American Studies, Howard University

Illustrations by Michael Bryant

❖ *Great African Americans Series* ❖

ENSLOW PUBLISHERS, INC.

Bloy St. & Ramsey Ave.	P.O. Box 38
Box 777	Aldershot
Hillside, NJ 07205	Hants GU12 6BP
U.S.A.	U.K.

To Alfreda Vance

Library of Congress Cataloging-in-Publication Data

McKissack, Pat, 1944–
    Madam C.J. Walker : self-made millionaire / Patricia and Fredrick
McKissack : illustrated by Michael Bryant.
        p. cm. — (Great African Americans series)
    Includes index.
    Summary: Describes the life of the black laundress who founded a
cosmetics company and became the first female self-made millionaire
in the United States.
    ISBN 0-89490-311-X
    1. Walker, C.J., Madam, 1867-1919—Juvenile literature. 2. Afro-
American women executives—Biography—Juvenile literature.
3. Women millionaires—United States—Biography—Juvenile
literature. 4. Cosmetics industry—United States—History—Juvenile
literature. [1. Walker, C.J., Madam, 1867-1919.
2. Businesswomen. 3. Afro-Americans—Biography.] I. McKissack,
Fredrick. II. Bryant, Michael, ill. III. Title. IV. Series: McKissack, Pat, 1944–
Great African Americans series.
HD9970.5.C672W356 1992
338.7'66855'092—dc20
[B]   92-6189
                                         CIP
                                       AC

Printed in the United States of America

10 9 8 7 6 5 4 3 2

Photo Credits: The Byron Collection, Museum of the City of New York, p. 22; From the
Walker Collection of A'Lelia Perry Bundles, pp. 4, 7, 15, 19, 24, 27, 28, 29; Library of Congress, pp. 17, 18.

Illustration Credit: Michael Bryant

Cover Illustration Credit: Ned O.

Contents

Madam C.J. Walker (Sarah Breedlove)
Born: December 23, 1867, Grand View Plantation, Louisiana.
Died: May 25, 1919, Irvington-on-Hudson, New York.

1

Christmas Baby

Before the Civil War, Owen and Minerva Breedlove were slaves. They worked in the cotton fields on a large Louisiana plantation. When the war ended in 1865, so did slavery. Millions of African Americans were freed, including the Breedloves and their two children, Alex and Louvenia.

Freedom was just about all the family had. Owen and Minerva did not have money, jobs, or a home. All they knew how to do was farm. But they had no land.

The Breedloves did what a lot of other slaves did. They became sharecroppers. They rented land from their old master and farmed it. Owen and Minerva worked long, hard hours on their rented farm. Still they stayed poor. Most of what they earned went to pay back the landowner for seeds and food. There was no way to get ahead.

Owen and Minerva Breedlove were going to have a third child. Christmas was not far away. There was no money for gifts. Two days before Christmas in 1867, Sarah Breedlove was born. The family called her their Christmas baby. They had high hopes for this child. She was born free!

Madam C.J. Walker was born Sarah Breedlove in this one-room cabin on a cotton plantation in Louisiana.

2

Moving up the River

Life was hard for Sarah and her family. It got even worse in 1874. Her parents died of yellow fever. Yellow fever is a disease carried by mosquitos. It killed many people in the South between 1874 and 1878.

Sarah's brother and sister, Alex and Louvenia, took care of her as best they could. But the cotton crops failed year after year.

Alex decided to go out West. Louvenia

and Sarah moved across the river to
Vicksburg, Mississippi. The two young
women took in laundry to make a living.
Both soon married. Young Sarah married
Moses McWilliams so she could "have a
home of her own." On June 6, 1885,
Sarah's daughter Lelia was born. Two
years later, Moses died.

Vicksburg was a river town. Sarah watched riverboats float up and down the river night and day. She decided it was time to move on, too. Sarah moved to St. Louis, Missouri in 1888.

Soon Sarah had a good laundry business there. But she wondered if life would ever be better for her and Lelia.

Sarah worked hard so Lelia could go to school. Lelia was bright and enjoyed reading. Sarah sent her to Knoxville College in Tennessee. Meanwhile, Sarah wasn't happy doing laundry. She wanted to do more with her life.

In 1904, Sarah went to hear Mrs. Margaret Murray Washington speak at a meeting of the National Association of Colored Women in St. Louis. Mrs. Washington was the wife of Booker T. Washington, the most well known black leader of the time. Mrs. Washington gave a great speech about the rewards of hard work.

Sarah made up her mind. She was going to improve her life.

3

The Walker Plan

There were not many products for black women's hair problems. Sarah's hair was thin and dry. So Sarah decided to make a hair grower to use on her own hair. It worked. Her hair grew longer and thicker.

Lelia was away in college. Sarah had married again, then divorced her husband. There was nothing keeping Sarah in St. Louis. So she moved to Denver where her brother's family lived. Her brother had died earlier.

Sarah got a job in a drug store. At night she worked on her hair products. Soon, Sarah began selling her goods from door to door. Black women were happy to have something that made their hair look nice. Sarah's sales were so good, she hired women to help sell door to door, too.

Sarah had known Charles Joseph Walker back in St. Louis. Now he lived in Denver, too. Their friendship grew into love. On January 4, 1906, Charles and Sarah were married. From that time on, she called herself Madam C.J. Walker.

Mme. C. J. Walker

The above cut represents Mme. Walker before and after her wonderful discovery.

Headquarters : Indianapolis, Ind., New York Office ; 108 West 136th Street
Atlantic City Office : 25 N. Indiana Ave., Brooklyn Office : 300 Bridge Street.
Please direct all mail to New York Office to Lelia W. Robinson.

Sarah's husband C.J. helped with advertising. This ad was for Madam Walker's Wonderful Hair Grower. Sarah and C.J. were divorced in 1912.

4

The Walker Team

When Lelia graduated from college, she came to help her mother. In 1908, Sarah and Lelia opened Lelia Beauty College in Pittsburgh, Pennsylvania. They trained women in the Walker hair care plan. Women who graduated from Madam Walker's school were called hair culturists.

First the culturist washed the woman's hair. Madam Walker's hair grower was added. Then the customer's hair was pressed with a hot comb and curled.

Madame Walker Giving a Manicure

Madam Walker trained women to have a "complete" look: well-groomed hair, well-pressed and clean clothing, and manicured hands.

In 1910, Madam Walker decided to build her first factory in Indianapolis, Indiana. Right away Madam Walker hired people to help build a strong business. Two lawyers, Robert Lee Brokenburr and Freeman Briley Ransom managed the company.

Madam C.J. Walker's first factory was located in Indianapolis, Indiana. She was 44 years old when she incorporated her company. Very few people knew how Madam Walker made her products.

Violet Davis Reynolds was Madam Walker's secretary and good friend. They traveled together. They showed other black women that they could start businesses, too.

Black women loved the idea! In 1910, most black women made from $2 to $10 a week. Madam Walker's hair culturists were making $20 a week or more.

Madam Walker enjoyed automobiles. She owned several. Although she had a driver, she sometimes drove herself.

A year after moving to Indianapolis, the company had 950 salespeople. The company earned $1,000 a month. Madam Walker put the money back into the business. By 1918 the company was earning $250,000 a year. Madam Walker made history by becoming America's first female self-made millionaire—white or black!

5

For a Good Cause

Lelia married and changed her name to A'Lelia. The marriage ended, but she kept the name A'Lelia Walker Robinson. A'Lelia didn't have any children of her own. So she adopted Mae Bryant, a young girl who worked at the Walker factory. She had long, thick hair. She became the model for the Walker Company.

Madam Walker used her money to make life better for her family and the people who worked for her. She also gave freely

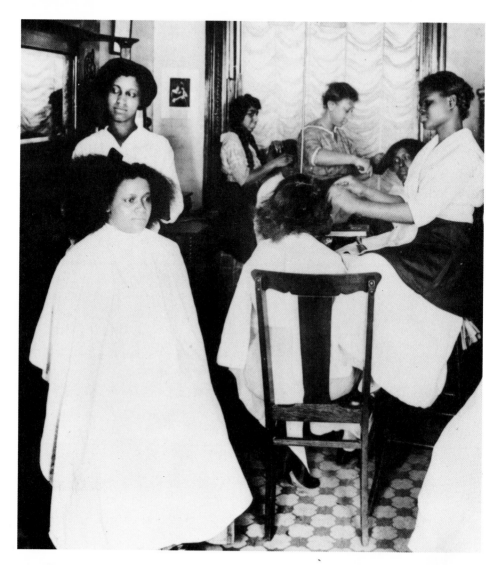

The three major products used in Madam Walker's salons were a hair grower, a vegetable shampoo, and Glossine, a light oil used to give hair sheen. A'Lelia is seated front left and her daughter Mae is standing rear left.

to churches, schools, hospitals, children's homes, and other good causes.

Madam Walker and A'Lelia were always interested in civil rights. At that time the country was segregated. This meant that laws kept black people and white people apart. Blacks and whites couldn't ride a bus or train together. They couldn't go to the same schools.

Madam Walker was known for giving donations to causes that helped her race. Here she is standing in front of Indianapolis's new black YMCA that was built in 1913. On the right of Madam Walker is Booker T. Washington, the president of Tuskegee Institute in Alabama. Standing in the rear (left) is her lawyer, manager, and friend, F.B. Ransom.

Once Madam Walker went to a white
theater. They charged her more money
because she was black. First, she sued the
theater. Then she built the Walker
Building, a block-long business center in
downtown Indianapolis. Inside, there was
a new movie theater where black and
white people could sit together.

Most jobs weren't open to blacks. Madam Walker spoke to groups all over the country. She believed black people needed to start more businesses in their own neighborhoods. Then there would be more jobs for other African Americans.

In 1913 A'Lelia moved to Harlem, a mostly black neighborhood in New York City. She wanted her mother to move the business there. Harlem was becoming the center of black life.

Finally, Madam Walker agreed that New York was the place to live. In 1916 she left Indianapolis. But the Walker Factory stayed there. F.B. Ransom and Alice Kelly were left in charge. Ms. Kelly knew Madam Walker's secret formula. Madam Walker and A'Lelia were the only other people who knew the formula at that time.

Villa Lewaro was—and still is—an impressive mansion overlooking the Hudson River in New York. The Walkers had big parties, picnics, and celebrations like the one above.

Madam Walker had worked hard all her life. Now her health was poor. Her doctors warned her to slow down, but she did not know how to rest. Madam Walker traveled around the country giving speeches and opening new shops.

Sarah Breedlove Walker died on May 25, 1919. She was 51 years old.

A'Lelia stayed in New York. She used her great wealth to help struggling black authors, artists, and musicians in the 1920s. In 1931 she died at age 46.

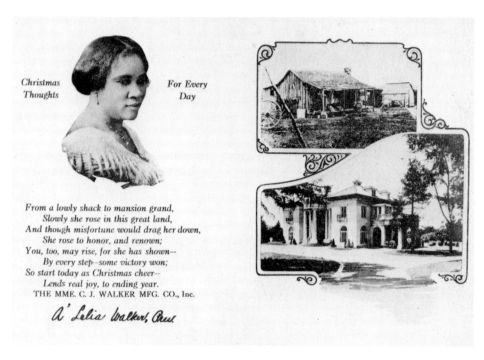

Christmas Thoughts

For Every Day

From a lowly shack to mansion grand,
Slowly she rose in this great land,
And though misfortune would drag her down,
She rose to honor, and renown;
You, too, may rise, for she has shown--
By every step--some victory won;
So start today as Christmas cheer--
Lends real joy, to ending year.
THE MME. C. J. WALKER MFG. CO., Inc.

A' Lelia Walker, Pres.

Madam C.J. Walker was an inspiration to many people. Although she was born a sharecropper's daughter, she died one of the richest women in the United States—black or white.

After Madam Walker died, A'Lelia became a very wealthy woman. She enjoyed life to the fullest.

Words to Know

civil rights—The rights of a free people, including the right to vote.

Civil War—A war fought in the United States between Southern states and Northern states, from 1861 to 1865. When this war ended, so did slavery.

factory—A place where products to be sold are made. Madam Walker made her hair products at home until she built a factory in 1910.

graduate— To finish the required course of study at a school.

hair grower—A product of the Walker Company that relieved dandruff and other hair scalp disease. It helped the scalp so hair could grow, but it could not cure baldness.

Harlem— A mostly black neighborhood in New York City. In 1915 only a few black people were living in Harlem. Large numbers of African Americans moved to Harlem after World War I.

National Association of Colored Women—In 1896 several national groups of black women joined together under this name. They worked for equal rights for African Americans and women.

plantation—A large farm with hundreds of people who worked in the fields. Before 1863, Southern plantations used slaves, like Sarah's parents, to raise cotton and other crops.

secretary—A person who helps in the day-to-day work of a business or an individual.

segregated—Separated from, apart. At one time, the United States had separate schools for blacks and whites. The two races could not work together or share public facilities, like hotels, restaurants, restrooms, and so on.

self-made millionaire—Madam Walker was the first black woman to become very wealthy by earning money through her own business.

slaves—People who are owned by other people and forced to work without pay.

yellow fever—A disease that killed thousands of people in the late 1800s. It is carried by mosquitos.

Index